Walk and E

Thomas Hardy's Dorset

by Robert Westwood

Inspiring Places Publishing
2 Down Lodge Close
Alderholt
Fordingbridge
Hants.
SP6 3JA
www.inspiringplaces.co.uk

ISBN 978-0-9955964-3-6
Contains Ordnance Survey data © Crown copyright and database right (2011)

Front cover: Pentridge (Trantridge in Tess of the D'Urbervilles). Rear cover: Stinsford Church. All photographs by the author except bottom left pg 26 by Robert Hesketh.

Introduction - *A map of walk locations is on the inside rear cover.*

Thomas Hardy is Dorset's most celebrated writer. He was born there and lived there for much of his life, drawing inspiration from the rural landscape he named 'Wessex'. To many people his works provide defining and enduring descriptions of the beautiful countryside of Dorset and surrounding areas, and his love of Wessex is evident throughout his novels and many of his poems. However, it is worth remembering that his stories document the bleak realities of rural life in the early nineteenth century and a number of them caused a sensation when they were first published; previously the novel had been a vehicle for humour and romance. The settings in his novels were based on real places and scholars and enthusiasts over the years have taken pleasure in identifying the locations. Many of these are little changed since Hardy's time and the walks in this book are centred around the places that form an important part of his Wessex novels, and also the places where he lived and wrote. For Hardy the natural world was an important part of his stories, often forming as much of a 'character' as the humans involved. He travelled widely around Dorset and was a great walker; as you follow these routes you will see much of the Dorset countryside that inspired him. With many of the walks there are places nearby which also feature in Hardy's work or were important in his life; these have also been detailed and you may care to visit them as part of your day out.

Many readers will be familiar with Hardy's novels, but I felt it might be useful to give a brief description of ones featured in these walks. Perhaps, when they have discovered the wonderful landscapes visited in this book, those who are not familiar with them may be inspired to pick up a copy.

Notes
Each walk description details the length of the walk and the total ascent. None are physically very taxing but please go well prepared with walking boots, suitable clothing, waterproofs and drinking water. All follow public footpaths and you are strongly advised to use the Ordnance Survey Explorer (and Outdoor Leisure) maps indicated; the maps in the book are intended as rough guides. The paths used are easily seen on the OS maps. Parts of some of the routes may be muddy at times and it is wise to expect this if it has been raining. Please follow the Country Code and keep dogs on leads near livestock and on routes where there are cliffs. Finally, enjoy the beautiful countryside and coastline on these literary walks!

The Hardy Way
This 220 mile footpath was created by Margaret Marande to link places important in Hardy's life and works. Parts of it feature in some of the book's walks. See www.thehardyway.co.uk.

Evershot - *The Woodlanders and Tess of the D'Urbervilles.*
Distance: 6 miles, ascent: 750 feet. Map: OS Explorer 117.

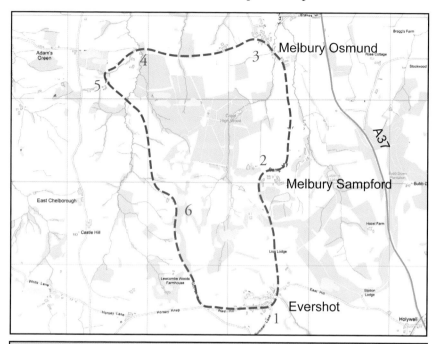

| Start: | Road junction and green at eastern end of village, ST 576047, nearest |

Start: Road junction and green at eastern end of village, ST 576047, nearest postcode DT2 0JY.
St Edwold's Church: Stockwood, DT2 0NG, ST 590069.
Melbury Bubb: DT2 0NQ, ST 596066.
Refreshments: The Acorn at Evershot. **Toilets:** None.

The setting of *The Woodlanders* is perhaps the part of Hardy's Dorset which has changed the least since his time. The novel charts the tangled love affairs between four main characters; Grace Melbury, a timber merchant's daughter, Giles Winterbourne, a woodsman, Dr Edred Fitzpiers and Felice Charmond, a monied widow. Still quite a heavily wooded landscape, Hardy's fictional locations like Great and Little Hintock were an amalgam of the pretty villages, churches and large houses dotted around this region. No one place can definitively claim to be either of these villages, but Melbury Osmond, through which the walk passes, is as unspoilt a Dorset village as you could hope to find, and as good an approximation of Great Hintock as any. Hardy's parents were married in its church and a copy of their wedding certificate hangs on a wall there. It may have been the model for Little Hintock church which features in the novel's closing passage. The lovely parkland of Melbury

Sampford House may also be the setting for Felice Charmond's house. The walk also includes places that feature in *Tess of the D'Urbervilles*. Evershot is Hardy's 'Evershead' and Tess's Cottage, on the corner of the road by the church, is where the heroine breakfasted on her way to try to see Angel Clare's parents and also the site of the barn where, on the way back, Tess heard Alec D'Urberville preaching. The popular Acorn pub features as the 'Sow and Acorn' in the novel.

1. From the starting point take the "Private Road", "footpath only" towards Melbury Sampford. Where the road forks keep left and follow this tarmac road through several gates as it sweeps round to the right at the back of Melbury Sampford House. You will see the estate offices and car park on your right.
2. Just after the car park follow the road as it turns left and continues through the park. Ignore the road to the right with a sign to the A37 and keep straight on. Pass through two wooden gates at the end of the estate and continue to follow the road through the village of Melbury Osmund.
3. Just before the church (you may want to visit this before continuing the walk) turn left along a lane signed "The Dairy House". At the end of the tarmac continue ahead on the "footpath". (It can be quite muddy here after rain.) Keep straight on ignoring footpath sign on your right. You will pass through several gates, keep straight ahead where the path passes another track.
4. When you reach a gate with a wood on your left continue through following the blue footpath marker. Go through the next gate at the bottom

Looking across to Evershot.

The village of Melbury Osmund.

of the field and follow the woodland path. (Again, it can be muddy here.) Next turn left towards the charming, small church at Lewcombe. Follow the path uphill away from the church, turning right in front of the manor house along a tree-lined avenue.

5. Just before the cottage on the left with the red post box turn left along the marked footpath. Go through a farm gate and follow the path across the field to the corner of a wood by a stream. Cross the stile into the wood, cross the stream (stepping stones) and over the stile on the other side. Go up the middle of the field heading for the right side of the wood ahead. Ignore the

Melbury Park.

first gate on the left and follow the left field boundary to the gate at the corner. Keep going through gates, across three more fields, heading diagonally uphill. The path becomes a clear track and as you approach Girt Farm, follow the path that goes to the left and above the farm.

6. Follow the path past Girt Farm, passing a deer park on your left. The path becomes a tarmac road and at the end of the deer park fencing take a footpath on the left. Keep the field boundary on your left, through a gate on the left marked "footpath", across the field and down to a stile in the centre of the hedge at the bottom. Go over this and turn right along the track between hedges. Turn left between trees along a dry stream bed to join a road. Turn right and follow the road to the church. Turn left down the street to the starting point. (Tess's Cottage is on your right as you join the main street.)

Tess's Cottage.

Melbury Bubb Church.

Stockwood Church.

Melbury Osmund Church.

Nearby

The lovely villages of **Stockwood** and **Melbury Bubb** also reputedly provided inspiration for the book's locations. The little church of **St Edwold** at Stockwood is Dorset's smallest and charmingly situated. Its unusual dedication indicates a connection with St Edwold, the Saxon hermit and nobleman who lived near the Silver Well at Cerne Abbas. Melbury Bubb is a tiny village off the beaten track at the foot of Bubb Down Hill, with a Jacobean manor next to another lovely old church.

Up Cerne - *Tess of the D'Urbervilles and The Woodlanders.*
Distance: 4.5 miles, ascent: 440 feet. Map: OS Explorer 117.

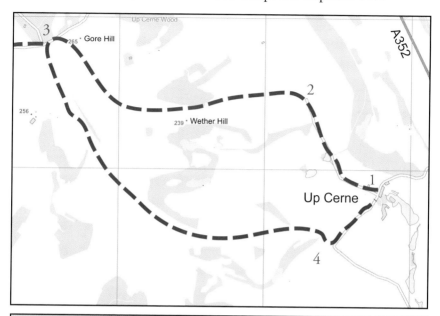

Start: ST 658028, DT2 7AW, at T-junction almost opposite entrance to Up Cerne House.
Cerne Abbey: At the end of Abbey Street, Cerne Abbas, DT2 7JQ. The Silver Well is at the far corner of the adjacent graveyard.
Minterne Gardens: In Minterne Magna, DT2 7AU, minterne.co.uk.
Refreshments: There are a number of pubs in Cerne Abbas, as well as the Abbot's Tearoom. **Toilets:** Public toilets in Cerne Abbas.

The manor at Up Cerne, near where the walk starts, is another candidate for the residence of Felice Charmond in *The Woodlanders*, but it is an important scene in *Tess of the D'Urbervilles* that is perhaps our dominant Hardy location. This is one of Hardy's most tragic novels and one that caused much public outrage. It tells the story of beautiful Tess Durbeyfield and her troubled relations with two men, Alec D'Urberville and Angel Clare, documenting what Hardy perceived as the iniquitous moral standards of the time. After going to try to see Angel Clare's parents in Emminster (Beaminster), Tess again stops in Evershead (Evershot) (see page 4) where she chances to hear a reformed Alec D'Urberville preaching in a barn. He glimpses her, catches her up and they talk. Alec leaves her at the Cross in Hand as he has another preaching engagement in Abbot's Cernel (Cerne Abbas), but before he does he makes her swear not to use her charms to tempt him again, putting her hand on the stone as she does so, telling her "This was once a Holy Cross." Tess continues her journey home along the top of the Chalk escarpment.

The Cross in Hand (below) is a stone pillar by the roadside. It may date from Roman times and was possibly originally a boundary marker of some sort. In Hardy's poem (see next page) the priest loses the pyx (a silver box with the sacrament) but later finds it in an illuminated spot surrounded by cattle. He erected the pillar to mark the place.

1. From Up Cerne follow the road up past the white house on the right. Continue past the pond and then shortly after take the footpath on the left signed "Wether Hill".
2. Follow this all the way to the top of the hill and then at a junction of paths turn right signed "Hillfield Hill".

3. When you reach the road turn left and follow it until you reach the Cross in Hand. Retrace your steps along the road and then turn right down a path opposite the road to Hillfield Priory signed "To the Wessex Ridgeway". Go past a path on the left to Wether Hill and shortly after fork left on a path signed "Up Cerne".
4. At the bottom of the hill where it joins the road turn left and follow it through the double avenue of trees back to Up Cerne and the starting point.

Walking down towards Up Cerne.

Nearby

A little way from Up Cerne is **Cerne Abbas (Abbots Cernel)**, famous for the figure of the giant cut into the Chalk hillside. Less well known are the charming remains of the old abbey and the Silver Well at the corner of the churchyard. The abbey features in Hardy's poem "The Lost Pyx" about a priest who sets off from the abbey to minister to a dying shepherd on the Chalk downs. The remains of the Benedictine Cerne Abbey from where the priest sets out are small but charming. The abbey was founded in 987 AD and the Abbot's Porch and Guesthouse both date from the fifteenth century. The Silver Well has a lovely story associated with it; it is thought to be the place where St Edwold, a Saxon nobleman escaping from constant warfare, set up a hermitage after giving silver pennies to locals who showed him the spring.

    Minterne Magna claims to be another location that inspired Great Hintock in *The Woodlanders*. The manor here is the home of the Digby family and its wonderful landscaped gardens are open to the public.

The Abbot's Porch, Cerne Abbey.

Up Cerne Manor.

The Silver Well.

Hilton and Bulbarrow - *Tess of the D'Urbervilles* and the poem "Wessex Heights". Distance: 5.5 miles, ascent: 750 feet. Map: OS Explorer 117.

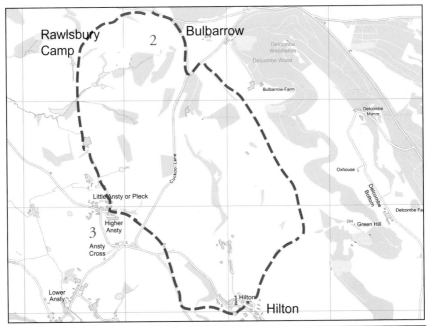

Start: By Hilton Church, DT11 0DG.
Milton Abbey: There is visitor parking at Milton Abbey School, DT11 0BZ. The abbey is open to visitors. Milton Abbas is a short distance away.
Refreshments: The Hambro Arms, Milton Abbas. **Toilets:** None.

The northern edge of the gently sloping Chalk strata is marked by a line of impressive escarpments. From the top of these, along which runs the ancient highway now known as the Wessex Ridgeway, spectacular views present over the fertile vales beneath. This again is the country of *Tess of the D'Urbervilles*, a novel which shocked the Victorian public and for which Hardy received much criticism. It was after this and a similar reception for *Jude the Obscure* that Hardy wrote the poem "Wessex Heights". The criticisms affected Hardy badly and he feels it is only on these hills that he can escape the pains and traumas of the human world.

There are some heights in Wessex, shaped as if by a kindly hand
For thinking, dreaming, dying on, and at crises when I stand,
Say, on Ingpen Beacon eastward, or on Wylls-Neck westwardly,
I seem where I was before my birth, and after death may be. ....

So I am found on Ingpen Beacon, or on Wylls-Neck to the west,
Or else on homely Bulbarrow, or little Pilsdon Crest,
Where men have never cared to haunt, nor women have walked with me,
And ghosts then keep their distance; and I know some liberty.
(first and last verses)

Tess journeys past Bulbarrow as she and her brother Abraham are taking beehives to market in Casterbridge (Dorchester). Hardy tells us it is "engirdled by its earthen trenches", presumably referring to the ramparts of the Iron Age hillfort of Rawlsbury Camp. Tess also passes this way when travelling home after hearing the news of her father's illness.

Looking towards Rawlsbury Camp and the Blackmore Vale.

1. Opposite the church take the footpath uphill signed "Bulbarrow". As you reach the top of the hill take the bridleway on the left through a small gate. At the next gate, go through and keep straight ahead. Keep following the path across the top of the downs with wonderful views to your left. You will reach a road, turn left here and at the next junction turn right, signed "Wooland" and "Hazelbury". Follow the road, keeping left where it joins a road from the right. There are lovely views all around here; to the right over the Blackmore Vale, Hardy's 'Vale of Little Dairies'.
2. You will soon see a footpath on the left signed "Dorset Gap". Take this, following the ramparts of the hillfort of Rawlsbury Camp. You are on the Wessex Ridgeway; follow this until you come to a 'crossroads' of paths at a field boundary. The ridgeway goes straight on, but turn left and follow the path down the field signed "Higher Ansty".

3. Go through a gate in the dip by a stream and copse and follow the track uphill past Rawlsbury Farm. Keep straight along what is now a tarmac road to Little Ansty. At a T-junction turn left and shortly after go through a gate ahead signed "footpath". Continue up through a gully between trees. At the top bear right across a field and head for a small gate which leads on to a road. Cross the road to a footpath directly opposite. Follow this diagonally across the next field towards some buildings. Go over the stile and turn right, again signed "footpath". Follow the track past farm buildings to another road. You can simply turn left here and follow the road back to Hilton and the starting point, or cross the road and take the bridleway across the field. At the end of the field turn left along the road for a short distance then take the bridleway on the left. Go across the field to a small gate and through it onto a woodland path. When you are level with the church to your left, take the path on the left through a gate and follow the path down to Hilton Church and the starting point. On your right you will see a lovely view of Milton Abbey.

Looking towards Higher Anstey.

Nearby
Milton Abbey is undoubtedly the 'Middleton Abbey' described in *The Woodlanders* as the temporary home of Felice Charmond (see page 3). The great house, now a school, was built in the mid-eighteenth century for Joseph Damer (also Baron Milton), although the abbey had been founded in 933 AD by King Athelstan. The abbey church, which was never finished, was started in the early fourteenth century. Damer disliked having the village near his great house and had it demolished and a new one built nearby. This is the picturesque Milton Abbas with its lines of near identical thatched cottages.

Portland - *The Well Beloved, The Trumpet Major (see page 26)*.
Distance: 5.5 miles, ascent: 600 feet. Map: OS OL15.

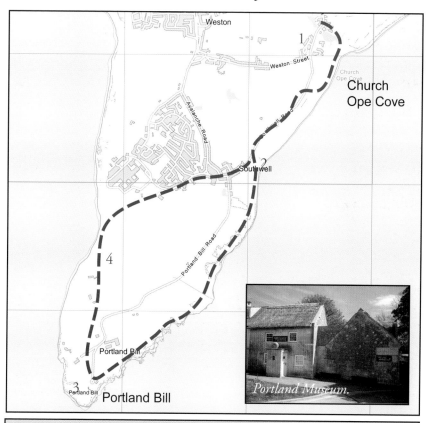

Portland Museum.

Start: By Portland Museum, Wakeham, DT5 1HS (free car park opposite). www. portlandmuseum.co.uk.
Refreshments: Portland Museum offers hot and cold drinks and ice creams. Various pubs en route but try The Lobster Pot cafe at Portland Bill for great sea views. **Toilets:** Portland Bill.

Our walk is very much at the heart of the locations Hardy used in his novel *The Well Beloved*. It centres around the character of Jocelyn Pierston, a renowned artist and son of a local stone merchant. He is consumed by a search for the ideal woman and the story deals with three short episodes in his life, each separated by twenty years, when he returns to Portland from London, and his relationships with a lady called Avice, her daughter Anne, and Anne's daughter, again called Avice. The first Avice lives in a cottage which Hardy based on our starting point, the Portland Museum. It was, incidentally, also the home of his friend, the pioneer of birth control, Marie Stopes. At one point in the story Jocelyn rents 'Sylvania Castle' which was based on Pennsylvania Castle very near the museum. Church Ope Cove is 'Ope Cove' where Hardy has granddaughter Avice and her lover Henri Leverre set off in a boat to elope and are subsequently rescued in the Race off Portland Bill. Anne and Isaac (later her husband) carve their names on the fallen stones of Rufus Castle (the 'Red King's Castle') above the cove.

Portland Bill.

1. Follow the path by the side of Portland Museum and after you pass under a small bridge turn right down the steps to Church Ope Cove. As you go down the steps you will see a sign to a ruined church; this is the church of St Andrew and was once the parish church of Portland. It's only a short detour to have a look. When you reach the bottom of the steps follow the path behind the beach huts. (You might want to spend some time in the cove first.) Keep going along the coast path and after a short while follow it as it zig-zags up to the road. Turn left along the road, keep going past Cheyne Weares car park and shortly after you will see a footpath sign on the left.
2. Take this and rejoin the coast path which you can follow all the way to Portland Bill.
3. After exploring Portland Bill go across the grassy area next to the MoD buildings and to the west of the main car park, then take the coast path.
4. At a stone marker just before some large buildings take the path to the right signed "East Cliff". Follow this path, keeping left when it appears to split (follow footpath signs). You will reach Sweethill Road where you should bear right and then right again after a little while. At the Eight Kings pub turn left at the mini-roundabout and follow the road back to the start.

Dorchester - *The Mayor of Casterbridge, Dorset County Museum, Hardy statue.* Distance: 2 miles, negligible ascent. Map: OS OL15.

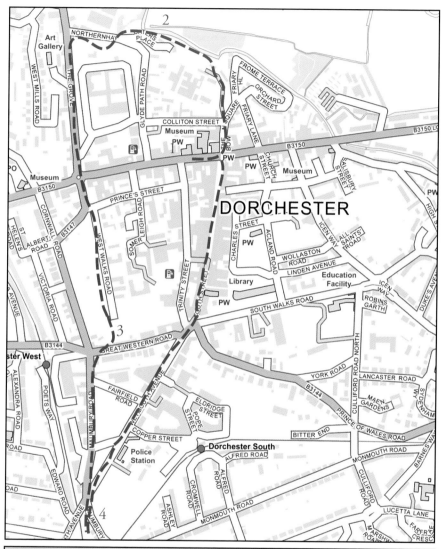

Start: By Dorset County Museum, High West Street, DT1 1XA, parking nearby in Acland Road car park, DT1 1EE.
Maiden Castle: DT2 9EY, 2 miles via road.
Dorset County Museum: www.dorsetcountymuseum.org.
Refreshments: Lots of pubs, restaurants and cafes in Dorchester.
Toilets: Acland Road car park.

The *Mayor of Casterbridge* tells the story of the rise and fall of Michael Henchard. It begins with him as an unemployed hay trusser who, after an argument, sells his wife and daughter at a fair while drunk. His wife, Susan, goes off willingly with the buyer, John Newsom, a sailor, and Henchard is almost immediately mortified at his own actions but, despite his efforts, he is not able to trace his wife and daughter. Nevertheless, he becomes a prosperous corn merchant and later mayor of Casterbidge. Susan and Elizabeth-Jane (John Newsom's daughter) eventually reappear and the story subsequently takes many twists and turns, also involving Henchard's business rival Donald Farfrae. It may appear to us rather far fetched to base a story around a wife being sold, but it seems that this was not an altogether unusual custom in England between the late-eighteenth and mid-nineteenth centuries. It was usually done by mutual consent as divorce was a prohibitively expensive procedure. Whilst not strictly legal, it was often ignored by courts.

Naturally there are a number of locations around Dorchester that feature in the story. The Corn Exchange is near the start of the walk; on the corner as you turn left down North Square. Just a short distance down the High Street from the museum is the King's Arms Hotel where Susan, having arrived back in Casterbridge, spies Henchard having dinner there. She sees him through the distinctive bay window that still survives. As you walk down North Square you will pass the old Dorchester prison, at the time of writing being converted into apartments. It was outside here that a sixteen year old Hardy witnessed his first public hanging, of Martha Brown, an attractive woman convicted of killing her bullying husband. It is thought she may have been in Hardy's thoughts when he wrote the story of *Tess of the D'Urbervilles*. A little while later the route passes 'Hangman's Cottage', formerly the home of the prison's official hangman. Maumbury Rings is an ancient Neolithic earthwork that was converted by the Romans to an amphitheatre. It features in the novel as a secret meeting place for Henchard and Susan after her return. As you head up South Street on the final part of the walk look out for Barclays

Maumbury Rings.

Hangman's Cottage.

Bank on your right; this was Henchard's house in the novel. Finally, we have the County Museum where you will find a reconstruction of Hardy's study at Max Gate, with the actual contents of that room.

1. From the Dorset County Museum on High West Street, walk a little way downhill and take the first left along North Square. Go past Colliton Street on the left and then fork left down Friary Hill. The old Dorchester Prison is on the hill to your left. Continue downhill and at the bottom turn left and follow the path alongside the stream.

2. When you reach a small footbridge keep left and continue along Northernhay; you will pass Hangman's Cottage on your right. You might like to visit the Roman Town House in the grounds of the council offices to your left. At the end of Northernhay turn left along The Grove and continue to the roundabout at the top. You will pass the statue of Thomas Hardy on the way. This was made by the renowned sculptor, Eric Kennington in 1931, and unveiled that year by J. M. Barrie. At the roundabout go straight across and then follow the West Walks path by the old town walls and Borough Gardens. A very small portion of the Roman town wall is still visible.

3. At the end of West Walks turn right and then almost immediately left along Maumbury Road. At the end cross over Weymouth Road and have a look at Maumbury Rings, originally a Neolithic henge that was transformed into a Roman amphitheatre.

4. From here turn right down Weymouth Road. At a junction of five roads go almost straight ahead along South Street; continue up as this becomes Cornhill and at the end you will arrive at the starting point.

The King's Arms.

The ramparts of Maiden Castle.

Nearby

It is about two miles from the starting point to **Maiden Castle**, so quite easy to walk there if you wish to extend the route. Just carry on past Maumbury Rings and shortly after turn right down Maiden Castle Road. This is a hugely impressive Iron Age hillfort and the **Dorset County Museum** has fascinating exhibits from the time it was taken by a Roman legion in 43 AD; including the vertebra of a defender with a Roman 'ballista' bolt still embedded in it. The castle, named 'Mai Dun' by Hardy, was where Henchard went to spy on Farfrae and Elizabeth-Jane. It also features in Hardy's short story "A Tryst at an Ancient Earthwork".

The Roman Town House.

Barclays Bank - the home of Michael Henchard.

Higher Bockhampton - *Hardy's birthplace and Under the Greenwood Tree.* Distance: 3.5 miles, ascent: 330 feet. Map: OS OL15.

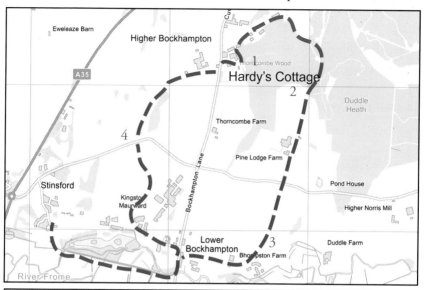

Start: Car park at Hardy's Cottage, DT2 8QJ, SY 728926.
Max Gate: DT1 2AB, SY 705898.
Stinsford Church: Parking at DT2 8PT, SY 712910, 2 miles via road.
Athelhampton House: DT2 7LG, 4 miles via road. athelhampton.co.uk.
Kingston Maurward: Parking for gardens at DT2 8PX, 2 miles via road.
Refreshments: Hardy's Cottage Visitor Centre, Pine Lodge Tea Rooms.
Toilets: Hardy's Cottage Visitor Centre.

Hardy's great grandfather built this cob and thatch cottage in 1800, and it was here in 1840 that Hardy was born. He lived here with his family until his marriage to Emma Gifford at the age of thirty-four. The cottage has changed little since and the furniture, although not that of the family, is from that time. It was here that Hardy wrote two of his most popular novels, *Under the Greenwood Tree* and *Far from the Madding Crowd*. The former is set in this immediate area and concerns the fortunes of the local, Mellstock church choir and the romantic entanglements of the young and beautiful village schoolmistress, Fancy Day. Mellstock was another of Hardy's composite locations, but Stinsford Church is undoubtedly Mellstock Church. Hardy's father played violin in the choir here and the book recounts how the musicians who played from the gallery were replaced by an organ played by the schoolmistress. There is a relatively new musicians' gallery in Stinsford Church, a gift from an American scholar.

Hardy's Cottage.

Lower Bockhampton certainly provided some inspiration for Mellstock and the bridge here features as Mellstock Bridge. We pass Hardy's schoolhouse as we turn towards Kingston Maurward from the main street. Note the school bell still over the front porch. Hardy visited Kingston Maurward House many times in his youth and he was taught by the wife of the owner of the house. It featured as 'Knapwater House' in his novel *Desperate Remedies*. Its gardens are open to the public.

DORSET
ANY PERSON WILFULLY INJURING
ANY PART OF THIS COUNTY BRIDGE
WILL BE GUILTY OF FELONY AND
UPON CONVICTION LIABLE TO BE
TRANSPORTED FOR LIFE
BY THE COURT
7&8 Geo 4 C30 S 9   T FOOKS

The bridge at Lower Bockhampton.

1. The walk starts at the car park for Hardy's Cottage. Walk along the lane to the cottage and carry on past it, but then immediately turn right. At the next signpost take the path to the left signed "Black Heath". At the next sign, with a pond on your right, go through a gate signed "Black Heath". Go straight on at the next gate which is just after a gate on the left signed "to Roman Road". (You might want to explore this a little before continuing. In fact the course of the Roman road runs roughly at right angles to the path you are on; so the straight tracks you see to the left and right are the Roman road!)

2. After a short while you will see a sign to Lower Bockhampton; take this and go straight on through another gate (with picnic table nearby) and through two farm gates. Pine Lodge Tea Rooms will be on your right. After another gate cross the road and follow the path signed "Lower Bockhampton".

3. At Bhompston Farm turn right at a T-junction, through a gate and shortly after turn left taking a footpath signed "Lower Bockhampton". Go across the field, over a stile and through a kissing gate. Head towards farm buildings, go through a kissing gate and through a number of gates through a farm. Follow the tarmac path past a number of houses and at the road turn right. Walk up the road a little way then turn left by a playground. (You might want to turn left at the road initially to view the interesting bridge (see picture)). Continue through the entrance to Kingston Maurward College, turn right past the Tudor manor house (signed "bridleway"). Go past the riding stables and take the bridleway sign on the left through a small wooded area. Keep straight on through two gates, across a gravel road (public bridleway).

Kingston Maurward House.

4. When you come to a road go straight across and then turn right immediately, following signs to "Hardy's Birthplace Visitor Centre". Go through another gate and follow the fence on your left to another gate at the top of the field. Follow the signs to the visitor centre and turn left when you reach the road. Follow the signs back to the visitor centre car park.

Note: To visit Stinsford Church and the Hardy family graves, take the footpath on the south side of the river just after the bridge. Follow this all the way to Stinsford and then retrace your steps to rejoin the walk route.

Max Gate.

Stinsford Church.

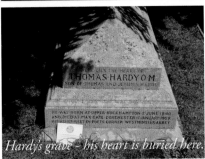
Hardy's grave - his heart is buried here.

Athelhampton House.

Nearby

Max Gate is the house Hardy designed and had built for him and his wife. They moved there in 1885 and Hardy lived there until his death in 1928. Emma died in 1912 and Hardy married his secretary Florence Dugdale. Like the cottage, Max Gate is looked after by the National Trust; it was bequeathed to them by Hardy's sister with the stipulation that it be lived in. It is offered to young scholars of Hardy while they complete their work on the author.

The wonderful fifteenth century manor, **Athelhampton House**, is just outside Puddletown. Hardy visited here many times and his father, a stonemason, worked on the house. Hardy was visiting Athelhampton when news of the outbreak of war was announced in 1914. He set the poem "The Dame of Athelhall" here. Athelhampton is open to the public.

Sutton Poyntz - *The Trumpet Major.* Distance: short loop (1-4) 3.5 miles, ascent: 530 feet; full walk 7 miles, ascent:1150 feet. Map: OS OL15.

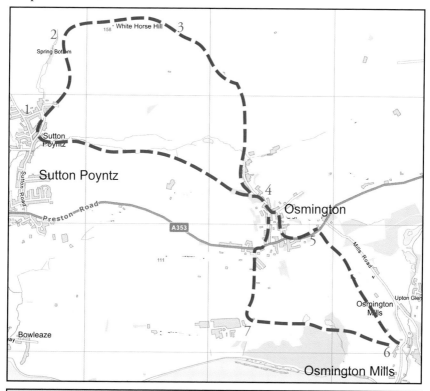

Start: By the Springhead pub in Sutton Poyntz, DT3 6LW, SY707838.
Portesham: DT3 4ET, about 9 miles by road from start.
Weymouth Old Harbour: DT4 8TJ, about 4 miles from start.
Refreshments: The Springhead at start or Smugglers' Inn, Osmington Mills. **Toilets:** Osmington Mills.

The Trumpet Major is set around Weymouth during the Napoleonic wars, when the threat of invasion was very real. The story centres around the fortunes of Anne Garland, the daughter of an impoverished but genteel widow. They live in part of miller Loveday's mill in the village of Overcombe (based on Sutton Poyntz). The sweet and gentle Anne has three suitors, the miller's two sons; Bob, a 'devil may care' and attractive sailor; John, a solid military man and the 'Trumpet Major'; and Festus Derriman, the nephew of the local squire and a thoroughly unlikeable character. The walk takes in the South Dorset Ridgeway where the villagers go to watch the arrival of King

The White Horse.

George's party as they pass along the road to Weymouth, and where John Loveday's regiment of dragoons sets up camp at the beginning of the novel. It is also the site of the White Horse, a representation of King George on horseback cut into the Chalk hillside. In the story Anne and John Loveday go to see it being made. There are splendid views over Weymouth, Hardy's 'Budmouth', from the ridgeway as well as Portland, where Anne stands on the Bill and watches Bob Loveday sail away on HMS *Victory*. (see page 14).

1. The walk begins by The Springhead pub in Sutton Poyntz. Walk past the pub to the end of the road and turn right along the footpath. Go through two gates, ignoring the first footpath sign on the left, and immediately after the second gate turn left at a junction and follow the path uphill between hedges. Go through a gate and continue up round the side of the hill – you will shortly come to a seat with lovely views over Weymouth and Portland.
2. Turn right here to White Horse Hill along the South Dorset Ridgeway. Go through a gate by a barrow and you will see a sign to the White Horse on the right. You can go down the hill here to have a closer look at this figure if you wish. Continue along the Ridgeway, through another gate and turn right to Osmington (still on the Ridgeway).
3. This path leads downhill to the village and when you come to a tarmac road at the bottom, turn right. Continue along the road and you will soon find an old village pump on the right. Here there is a path on the right signed to Sutton Poyntz.
4. If you don't want to do the extended walk take this path back to the start

point (see later description), otherwise continue up the road until you reach a junction. Turn left along Village Street (signed "Osmington Mills") and follow the road up Chapel Lane. At the main road turn left. Just after Craig's Farm Dairy you will see the South Dorset Ridgeway path signed on the right.

5. Go through the gate and follow the path to the left of the field. Go through the next kissing gate, continue uphill and through the next kissing gate. Still following the signs to Osmington Mills the path goes between telegraph poles and through another gate where the path keeps to the left of the field and leads towards cottages. Go through the kissing gate at the bottom and then turn immediately right along the coast path. If you wish, before you do this, keep straight on to the road and have a look at the beach at Osmington Mills and perhaps visit the well known Smugglers' Inn, once the haunt of the French smuggler Pierre Latour.

6. Back on the coast path continue over a number of stiles following the South West Coast Path signs to Weymouth. You will reach a gate which the

The path down to Osmington.

coast path goes through to the left. Do not take this but follow the path to the right of this to Osmington. Go over a stile, through a gate and follow the path to another stile by a signpost.

7. Go over the stile and turn right along the tarmac road, following this to the main road. Turn right and then next left down Church Lane. Continue down the road until you reach the village pump mentioned earlier.

4. Take the track to the left here towards Sutton Poyntz. When this track makes a right turn signed "Private" go through two gates opposite and across the field. You will cross a track via two stiles and continue across the next

field. Go over another stile and continue on the path with the hedge on your right. It may be a bit boggy here so you might want to go across higher up the field if it is too wet. Continue along this path through a gap in the hedge. Go across a track and through a gate opposite. The path bears right and just before another five bar gate turn left through a small gate signed "footpath". Go through a kissing gate and follow the path between houses until you come to the road. Turn right back to the starting point.

Osmington Mills.

Sutton Poyntz.

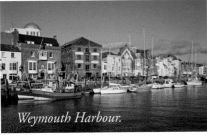
Weymouth Harbour.

The Esplanade, Weymouth.

Nearby

As we have noted, **Weymouth** features as 'Budmouth' in Hardy's novels and *The Trumpet Major* is set at the time when holidaying beside the sea was being promoted by King George III who found his regular visits here were beneficial to his health. Hardy came here in 1869 as an architect's assistant and reputedly enjoyed bathing and rowing in the bay. It was also the scene of a brief, youthful dalliance with his cousin Tryphena. The impressive Georgian seafront is much as it was in Hardy's time, as is the old harbour.

The village of **Portesham** features in the novel in its true setting as the home of Thomas Masterman Hardy, Nelson's flag captain on HMS *Victory* at the Battle of Trafalgar. In the story, Bob Loveday goes to visit Captain Hardy here to enlist on the *Victory*. The Hardy monument on the nearby Black Down Hill was built to commemorate him and to serve as a marker for shipping. Its shape represents the sort of telescope Hardy would have used at sea. Hardy's house can be seen from the road out of the village towards Abbotsbury.

Lulworth - *Far From the Madding Crowd, The Distracted Preacher.*
Distance: 4 miles, ascent: 920 feet. Map: OS OL15.

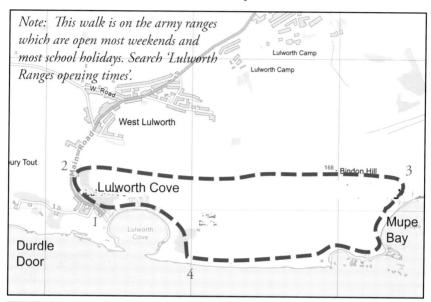

> *Note: This walk is on the army ranges which are open most weekends and most school holidays. Search 'Lulworth Ranges opening times'.*

Start: The Heritage Centre car park, BH20 5RQ.
Durdle Door: Walk westwards up track from car park or park at BH20 5PU (Durdle Door Holiday Park).
Refreshments: A wide choice in Lulworth Cove, also Weld Arms in East Lulworth, BH20 5QQ. **Toilets:** Lulworth Cove.

For almost all of this walk you will enjoy spectacular views over Lulworth Cove, Mupe Bay, Mupe Rocks and across Weymouth Bay to the Isle of Portland, Hardy's 'Isle of Slingers'. The unique cove is the result of wave erosion scouring the softer rocks between the harder strata of Chalk and the Portland and Purbeck limestones. This was made possible after a river, swollen with glacial meltwater, punched through the limestones at the end of the last Ice Age. Lulworth features as 'Lulwind Cove' in *Far From the Madding Crowd* and Hardy's short story of smuggling, *The Distracted Preacher*, where it is the location smuggled brandy is unloaded. *Far From the Madding Crowd* centres around the strong minded heroine, Bathsheba Everdene. Genial shepherd Gabriel Oak falls in love with her but she rejects him. After she inherits a large farm she is pursued by a neighbouring wealthy landowner and a dashing but fickle soldier, Sergeant Troy, whom she marries. One night Sergeant Troy goes for a swim at 'Lulwind' and gets into trouble after swimming out of the cove -

"Troy presently swam between the two projecting spurs of rock which formed the pillars of Hercules to this miniature Mediterranean."

Lulworth was also the setting for Hardy's poem "At Lulworth Cove a Century Back", written to celebrate the poet John Keats who, it is thought, spent his last night in England there in September 1820 as his ship was becalmed en route to Rome where he died five months later.

"Had I but lived a hundred years ago
I might have gone, as I have gone this year,
By Warmwell Cross on to a Cove I know,
And Time have placed his finger on me there:"

Lulworth Cove.

1. From the main car park near the Heritage Centre turn left up the road, keeping to the footpath on the right hand side. At the end of the row of houses you will see a path on the right signed "Bindon Hill".

2. Take this and climb up to the top of the hill. Continue in the same direction (east) along the grassy path on the crest of the ridge. You will pass a small radar station; continue in the same direction along a chalky path, keep left where the path forks, do not take the path that descends to the coast. Follow the path until it nearly reaches the steep Chalk cliffs.

3. You will see a path on your right that steeply descends towards Mupe Bay. Take this path down to the edge of Mupe Rocks and then follow the coast path to the right back towards Lulworth Cove. Keep going on the coast path; this is still part of the army ranges and is clearly signposted. You will

go through a gate at the end of the ranges; keep going towards Lulworth and you will be rewarded by a wonderful view over the cove.

4. Just before it reaches the edge of the cove there is a path on the right; take this and where it bends round to the right take the small path on the left that descends to the cove. Walk around the cove on the beach back to the road and the car park. Note you will not be able to do this at high tide, so please check tide times beforehand. The walk can be done the other way round, but the climb up Bindon Hill from Mupe Bay is very tiring!

Nearby

In the latest film version of *Far From the Madding Crowd* starring Carey Mulligan as Bathsheba, some scenes were filmed at **Durdle Door**. Near the beginning Bathsheba is seen leaving her cottage on the way to the farm she has inherited and drives along the coast path above Durdle Door. A bay near here was also used for Sergeant Troy's swim out to sea, instead of neighbouring Lulworth. **Man O' War Bay** is on the eastern side of Durdle Door and is actually quite a safe place to swim, with a ridge of limestones helping to calm the inner waters of the bay.

Durdle Door.

Mupe Rocks.

Man O' War Bay.

Sturminster Newton - *Hardy's home by the River Stour.* Distance: 3.5 miles, negligible ascent. Map: OS Explorer 129.

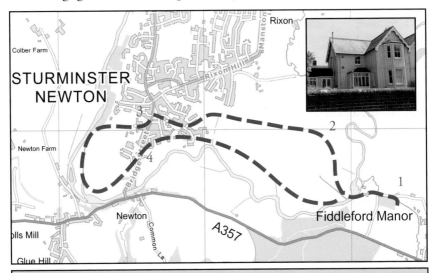

> **Start:** Car park next to Fiddleford Manor, DT10 2BX.
> **Marnhull:** Approximately 5 miles from Fiddleford Manor, church at DT10 1PZ. The Crown is very nearby. Tess' cottage DT10 1NH, ST780179. **Refreshments:** A wide choice in Sturmister, The Crown, Marnhull. **Toilets:** Sturminster Newton.

Riverside Villa, which Thomas Hardy rented from July 1876 to March 1878, is a substantial house overlooking the River Stour. Hardy brought his new bride, Emma, to the villa and he regarded their stay here as the happiest period of their married life. It was in Sturminster that Hardy wrote *The Return of the Native*; working with Emma who did his note taking. After Emma's death, which affected him deeply, Hardy visited Sturminster Newton again and wrote the poem "Overlooking the River Stour", which perhaps expresses some of his regret at their estrangement in the last years of her life.

1. Exit the small, grassy car park for Fiddleford Manor and turn left down the small lane. Turn left at the bottom and walk past the mill to the river. Cross the river on the footbridge and turn right, following the river bank until you reach the old, disused railway line.

2. Turn left on the embankment and follow the track towards the town. Just before the town a number of footpaths converge. Take the first on the left and follow the path along the side of a field. At the end of the field turn right and follow the track to a road (Penny Street); turn right and follow it into

town. Proceed to the main street (B3092) and turn left. Continue down the road until you reach Ricketts Lane on the right (just after the White Hart on your left).

3. Go down this lane, past the sports field to the river. The villa where Thomas Hardy lived is on your right, easily recognisable from the photograph (inset map). Turn left on the path next to the river and follow it down to the mill. Here keep left and continue to follow the river to the bridge and the road into Sturminster Newton. At the road turn left and follow it a little way until you see a path on the right.

4. Take this and follow it round to where it meets Church Lane. Turn right and follow the road past the church. Keep to the right (south) of the church along Church Walk and you will meet Penny Street again where you can shortly turn right along the path you used before. When you reach the field keep right and follow the footpath across the meadow by the river until you reach the footbridge. Cross the river and return to the starting point.

The bridge over the River Stour.

Nearby

The large village of **Marnhull** was 'Marlott' in *Tess of the d'Urbervilles* and was the location of the Durbeyfield family home. Tess' Cottage is a gorgeous grade II listed seventeenth century thatched cottage that was reputedly the model for Tess' home. It is now in private ownership but can be seen from the road. The village pub, The Crown, was 'The Pure Drop' of the novel where Tess' father had been drinking before meeting the vicar who told him of his connection with the ancient d'Urberville family. The pub is popular with Hardy fans and retains a cosy, traditional feel.

Bere Regis - *The Return of the Native, Far From the Madding Crowd* and *Tess of the D'Urbervilles.* Distance: 3.5 miles, ascent: 450 feet. Map: OS Explorer 117.

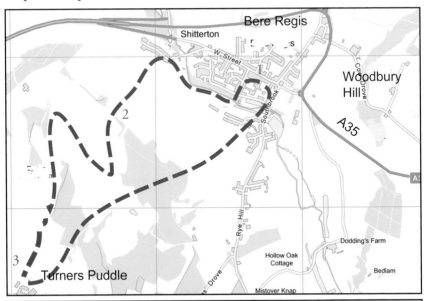

Start: Turberville car park in middle of Bere Regis, BH20 7LZ.
Woolbridge Manor: About 5 miles south of Bere Regis on the road to Wool. Can be seen from the old bridge over the River Frome.
SY844872, nearest postcode BH20 6DP (Wool Station).
Woodbury Hill: Accessed from Cow Drove near A31/A35 roundabout.
Refreshments: Bere Regis has the Drax Arms and the Royal Oak Hotel.
Toilets: None.

Bere Regis was once part of the manor owned by the Turberville family, descendants of a knight who came over with William the Conqueror in 1066. In *Tess of the D'Urbervilles*, John Durbeyfield, Tess' father, is told, in the opening scene, that he is a descendant of this ancient family by the local vicar who has been researching them. Members of the real Turberville family are buried in the huge family vault under the floor of the Turberville Chapel in the south aisle of St John the Baptist Church, Bere Regis, and a number of stained glass windows commemorate those who have held manorial rights here which were originally granted by King John.

The Return of the Native revolves around the complicated lives and loves of two very different women. It is set entirely on 'Egdon Heath', Hardy's name for the once extensive Dorset heathland between Wimborne and Dorchester. Hardy's symbolic use of the landscape is perhaps never more pronounced than in this novel. He probably had in mind as the setting areas of the heath east of his home in Higher Bockhampton but the small area of heathland on our walk is one of the few places which resemble the ancient heathland that Hardy wrote about.

The view over Bere Regis.

The Turberville windows.

1. From the car park in the centre of the village turn left onto Manor Farm Road. Cross Elder Road and go over the footbridge across the stream. Immediately turn right through a gate onto Souls Moor and Bere Stream Nature Reserve (by notice board). You will shortly come to a bridge over the stream, do not cross but follow the path alongside the stream on the left. Where the path splits take the left fork and then turn left at a T-junction. Follow this path between hedgerows to the top.

2. It turns left where a track joins and is signposted "Jubilee Trail". Follow the path round to the right, still signed "Jubilee Trail". After rain some parts may be muddy. You will shortly come to Black Hill Heath and a T-junction; turn right, still following the Jubilee Trail. Continue along the track with lovely views over the valley; go through a five-bar gate and at a cross-roads with another track turn left (just before a barn) and follow this wide track all the way downhill (still Jubilee Trail) until you nearly reach Turners Puddle.

3. Just before a five-bar gate turn left along a marked footpath. Go through a gate, across a track, through the next gate and turn left along a bridleway. Continue uphill, through a five-bar gate. Ignore a path to the right but keep right at the top of the hill where the track forks. Go straight on at a crossroads and follow path downhill past a 'home made' play area. At the bottom left hand corner is a gate, go through this and follow the path between trees. You will emerge by Egdon Close. Continue down to the 'main' road and take the path to the church. When you have had a look at this wonderful church go through the back entrance to the churchyard and straight on past a few houses to the car park.

Nearby

Woolbridge Manor is a largely seventeenth century house once owned by the Turberville family. In *Tess of the D'Urbervilles* it is the ancestral home of Tess' distinguished forebears and Angel and Tess rent a room here for their ill-fated wedding night. **Woodbury Hill** just outside of Bere Regis was the site of an important medieval fair and Hardy used it as the setting for 'Greenhill Fair' in *Far From the Madding Crowd* where Bathsheba saw Sergeant Troy acting the part of Dick Turpin in a side show.

Woolbridge Manor.

Swanage - *The Hand of Ethelberta.* Distance: 6.5 miles, ascent: 770 feet. Map: OS OL15.

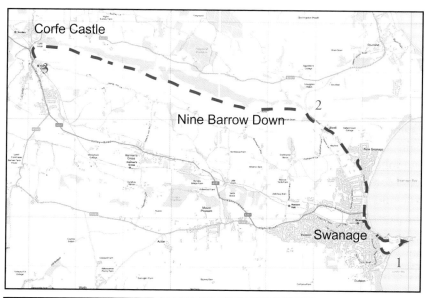

Start: Peveril Point, BH19 2AY, SZ041787. Large car park nearby.
Kingston: The Scott Arms at BH20 5LH. The car park (Sheep's Pen) for Swyre Head is at SY944793, follow road past church as far as it goes, car park is on left at the end.
Refreshments: A wide choice in Swanage and Corfe Castle or the Scott Arms in Kingston. **Toilets:** Swanage and Corfe Castle.

Hardy and his wife Emma stayed in Swanage in the summer and autumn of 1875 where he completed *The Hand of Ethelberta.* Ethelberta Petherwin is a young, society widow of humble origins, who four men want to marry. They are Christopher Julian, a musician; Eustace Ladywell, an artist, Mr Neigh; and the elderly Lord Edgar Mountclere. Ethelberta falls upon hard times and lives with her family in Knollsea (Swanage). Lord Mountclere invites Ethelberta to a meeting of an archaeological society in Corvsgate (Corfe Castle) and to save money she goes there by donkey, essentially along the route taken by our walk, over Nine Barrow Down. At the end of the journey she ties the donkey up while she goes for a look around the castle, prompting an amusing scene as other, more well to do guests, arrive in carriages. Swanage pier features in the story when Ethelberta catches a steamer from there to Cherbourg to visit her aunt in France. The historic paddle steamer *Waverley* still occasionally leaves Swanage pier for pleasure cruises along the Jurassic Coast.

This is a one way walk from Swanage to Corfe Castle along the Chalk ridge. Why not travel back on the famous steam railway?

1. We start at Peveril Point at the southern tip of Swanage Bay. In the *Hand of Ethelberta* Hardy says the steamer carrying Ethelberta steered easterly for a while to "...avoid a sinister ledge of limestones, jutting from the water like crocodile's teeth, ...". This ledge, clearly visible at low tide, is a small fold or syncline in the Purbeck strata. From here walk north to the seafront at Swanage and continue along it (Shore Road) until you come to Ulwell Road. Follow this out of the town towards Studland. Continue past Ulwell Farm Caravan Park and just past a layby on the right hand side of the road.
2. Turn left on a footpath to Nine Barrow Down which leads up onto the Chalk ridge. There is a footpath by the road almost all of the way to this point. Where it finishes there is a footpath alongside the road just behind the fence, although it can be a bit overgrown. Either take this or walk carefully along the road – it is only a short distance. Once on Nine Barrow Down follow the path along the top of the ridge all the way to Corfe Castle. Just before the village there is a path on the left leading down to the road. Follow this into the village.
3. The entrance to the station is down a small road almost opposite the square and the church. Trains back to Swanage are relatively frequent, check out the timetable at www.swanagerailway.co.uk or call 01929 425800.

Corfe Castle from East Hill.

Nearby

Lord Mountclere's estate, Enckworth Court, is based on Encombe House, a beautifully situated eighteenth century mansion in the **'Golden Bowl'** near the village of Kingston. You can get a great view of the estate and house by taking the footpath from Sheep's Pen car park (or walking there from Kingston) to Swyre Head, from where there are also perhaps the best views in Purbeck, across Kimmeridge Bay to the west and St Aldhelm's Head to the east. On the way back why not stop in the Scott Arms in Kingston. This was where Christopher Julian stopped for a drink in 'Little Enckworth'.

The view west from Swyre Head.

Walk up to Swyre Head from Sheep's Pen car park. Follow field boundary to the right on the west side of the headland to "Heaven's Gate". Turn right and follow path back to car park.

Sheep's Pen

Kingston

The Golden Bowl

Swyre Head

The Scott Arms.

The Golden Bowl.

Cranborne - *Tess of the D'Urbervilles.* Distance: 7.5 miles, ascent: 750 feet. Map: OS Explorer 118.

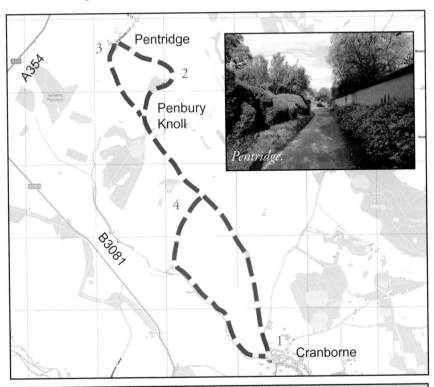

Pentridge.

Start: The Square, Cranborne, BH21 5PR.
Larmer Tree Gardens: near Tollard Royal, SP5 5PY, 9 miles from Cranborne, www.larmertree.co.uk.
Refreshments: The Inn at Cranborne (formerly the Fleur de Lys). The Sheath of Arrows in the Square, Cranborne. Cranborne Garden Centre has a cafe as does the Larmer Tree Gardens. **Toilets:** None.

We again find oursleves in the country of *Tess of the D'Urbervilles* on this walk, directly on the scene of one of the book's most dramatic and critical episodes. The D'Urberville family had given Tess employment and after a night out in Chaseborough (Cranborne) Tess walks home to Trantridge (Pentridge) with the other workers. Following an argument she finds herself alone but is 'rescued' by Alec D'Urberville who offers to escort her home. On the way he seduces the tired and exhausted Tess. She conceives a child and future hardships are guaranteed. Thus on this walk from Cranborne to Pentridge we follow in Tess' tragic literary footsteps.

The pub in Cranborne now known as 'The Inn at Cranborne' was, until a short time ago, called the 'Fleur de Lys'. Hardy called it the 'Flower de Luce' in the novel and it was here, on Saturday nights, that the workers from Trantridge would usually go. Trantridge itself was the location of the D'Urberville estate, but there is no grand house here which might have been a model for Hardy. The village is another where little has changed for many years. It lies on a cul-de-sac, remote and secluded, with a charming church and lovely village green.

1. Follow the road northwards out of the square at Cranborne (Salisbury Street) then shortly take the left fork signed "Boveridge". Keep going as the tarmac gives way to a gravel path. After about thirty minutes you will reach the junction at "Jack's Hedge Corner", carry straight on on what is now the Jubilee Trail. Carry on past a path on your left, still on the Jubilee Trail. Ignore a path over a stile on your right and you will come to a gate. Go through and keep straight on, ignoring the path on the left. You will shortly come to the Iron Age hillfort of Penbury Knoll, a good place to stop and admire the views. Go through a gate and carry on around the right (southern) side of the hill.

2. At the end of the woodland that covers the top of the hill turn left and down the side of the hill towards Pentridge. You will soon see a stile over a fence signed "Hardy Way". Go over this and follow the path across the field. Towards the bottom of the field follow the path round keeping the fence on your left then go over a stile and follow the straight path down to the road. You are now at Pentridge. Turn left and follow the road past Manor Farm.

The view towards Penbury Knoll.

(You might want to explore the village first; the church is worth seeing.)

3. At a pair of gates as the track turns right go through the left hand gate and along the path marked "Hardy Way". Keep going up the hill through another gate and at the top go through the gate on the left and rejoin the track you took up to Penbury Knoll. Carry on down until you reach Jack's Hedge Corner again.

4. Here turn right along the track and follow it down hill. At the farm buildings turn left and follow the track along the valley of the little River Crane. At the next farm buildings the track goes round to the right but turn left in front of the cottage, through the gate and follow the track across the field to Cranborne and the starting point.

Larmer Tree Gardens.

Nearby

The **Larmer Tree Gardens** lie about nine miles from Cranborne and provide another opportunity to step back into Hardy's world. The gardens were developed by Victorian philanthropist and pioneer of archaeology Augustus Pitt-Rivers for the enjoyment of estate workers and locals. Today they present much as they would have done when Hardy visited them with his wife, Emma in 1895. They were staying with Pitt-Rivers and enjoyed a sports-day and evening entertainment. The gardens were lit by hundreds of lanterns and Hardy described it as "Quite the prettiest sight I ever saw in my life". The philosophy remains the same; encouraging visitors to relax and enjoy a beautiful, tranquil, rural setting. They close for winter and a number of events are hosted here; please check the website for opening times.